Poetry

Comics

South African Library, Cape Town, document no. G.13.c.78 in the Grey Collection.

COLENSO, JOHN W. (1864). 'On Missions to the Zulus in Natal and Zululand', *Social Sciences Review*, June 1864. (Repr. B. W. Richardson, London. In the South African Library, document 575.e.1066 (10) of the Grey Collection.)

——(1872). *First Steps in Zulu: Being an Elementary Grammar of the Zulu Language*. (2nd edn.) Pietermaritzburg: P. Davis and Sons.

COMAROFF, JEAN (1985). *Body of Power, Spirit of Resistance: The Culture and History of a South African People*. Chicago: University of Chicago Press.

COMAROFF, JOHN, and COMAROFF, JEAN (1992). *Ethnography and the Historical Imagination*. Boulder, Col.: Westview Press.

COMMONWEALTH SECRETARIAT (1986). *Mission to South Africa: The Commonwealth Report of the Group of Eminent Persons*. Harmondsworth: Penguin Books.

CRAPANZANO, VINCENT (1985). *Waiting: The Whites of South Africa*. New York: Random House.

DOUGLAS, BRONWEN (1992). 'Doing Ethnographic History: The Case of Fighting in New Caledonia', in James G. Carrier (ed.), *History and Tradition in Melanesian Anthropology*. Berkeley, Calif.: University of California Press: 86–115.

FREUND, BILL (1984). *The Making of Contemporary Africa: The Development of African Society since 1800*. Bloomington, Ind.: Indiana University Press.

GLUCKMAN, MAX (1940). 'Analysis of a Social Situation in Modern Zululand', *Bantu Studies*, 14: 1–30.

HAMILTON, CAROLYN (1992). ' "The Character and Objects of Chaka": A Reconsideration of the Making of Shaka as "Mfecane" Motor', *Journal of African History*, 33: 37–63.

HUNTER, MONICA (Wilson) (1936). *Reaction to Conquest: Effects of Contact with Europeans on the Pondo of South Africa*. Oxford: Oxford University Press.

LABAND, JOHN (1992). *'Kingdom in Crisis': The Zulu Response to the British Invasion of 1879*. Pietermaritzburg: University of Natal Press.

MACMILLAN, W. M. (1963 [1929]). *Bantu, Boer and Briton: The Making of the South African Native Problem*. Oxford: Clarendon.

MARKS, SHULA (1986). *The Ambiguities of Dependence in South Africa: Class, Nationalism and the State in Twentieth Century Natal*. Johannesburg: Ravan Press.

MARTIN, RUSSELL (1984). 'The Zulu in the British Imagination', Ph.D. dissertation (Cambridge).

MORRIS, ALAN (1992). *Bones of Contention*. Johannesburg: Witwatersrand University Press.

MULLER, C. F. J. (ed.) (1981). *500 Years: A History of South Africa*. (3rd edn.) Pretoria: Academica.

OMER-COOPER, J. D. (1987). *History of Southern Africa*. London: James Curry.

RIVE, RICHARD, and COUZENS, TIME (1991). *Seme: The Founder of the ANC*. Johannesburg: Skotaville.

ROTBERG, ROBERT (1988). *The Founder: Cecil Rhodes and the Pursuit of Power*. New York: Oxford University Press.

THORNTON, ROBERT (1983*a*). 'Narrative Ethnography in Africa, 1850–1920: The Creation and Capture of an Appropriate Domain for Anthropology', *Man*, 18: 502–20.

——(1983*b*). 'The Elusive Unity of Sir George Grey's Library', *African Studies*, 42/1: 79–89.

WILSON, MONICA, and THOMPSON, LEONARD (1971). *The Oxford History of South Africa*, i: *South Africa to 1870*; ii: *South Africa, 1870–1966*. Oxford: Clarendon.

WRIGHT, JOHN (1989). 'Political Mythology and the Making of Natal's Mfecane', *Canadian Journal of African Studies*, 28: 272–91.

8

Hellenism and Occidentalism:
The Permutations of Performance in
Greek Bourgeois Identity

Michael Herzfeld

During a recent period of field research in the town of Rethemnos, on the north coast of the island of Crete,[1] a junior official of the local chamber of commerce asked me bluntly whether the Greeks were European or Oriental. When I tried to duck the question, which struck me as Hobson's choice between two equally unattractive and essentialist alternatives, I was told rather crossly that I was just offering diplomatic niceties, and asked again what I really thought. Nothing would persuade my interlocutor that I was not simply being evasive: it was clear that he suspected me of believing Greeks to be Oriental and of being too embarrassed to admit it. The conceptual reasons for my embarrassment meant nothing to him; the essentialism of state teleology had done its work far too well. The fact that I was unambiguously a 'Westerner' from his perspective probably only made matters worse. Virtually anything I might say would sound condescending; any answer would be primed to offend.

Encapsulated in this encounter was a tension that one meets repeatedly in Greece. The existence of a Greek nation-state was reluctantly predicated by the so-called Great Powers on the Greeks' presumed intellectual ancestry of European civilization; yet this genealogy was itself largely invented by Enlightenment philologists and historians, and the Greeks were constantly told, in the established tradition of imperial paternalism, to let their political elders and betters decide what parts of their present-day culture could legitimately be classified as 'Greek'.[2] In one of the most colossal pieces of global chutzpah ever perpetrated, the Greeks were effectively taught that whatever was most familiar in their everyday lives was probably of Turkish origin and therefore by definition 'foreign'. The local, largely occidentalized élite eagerly enforced this process of cultural cleansing, since its own relatively secure access to philological classicism—enshrined in its use of the puristic *katharvousa* (i.e. 'cleansed') language—gave it practical advantages to which it subsequently clung in the realistic assessment that this cultural etiquette also secured its monopoly of power and wealth (see Mouzelis 1978; Sotiropoulos 1977).

Yet doubts remained, even among the élite. Preaching the foreignness of all things local for a century and a half must eventually erode one's own claims on authenticity. To the extent that the élite colluded in the dismissal of its own country as a 'sad relic of departed worth', as Byron so aptly summarized the peculiar cultural historiography of a Greece caught between Levantine tawdriness and degenerated Hellenism, it inevitably ended up looking like a bit of a sad relic itself. Only the spread of full Hellenization could persuade foreign benefactors that the country was, after all, worthy of their support; and, without that support, the élite's own power was at risk. On the other hand, this education should not be too effective, because that would dilute the élite's power from within. Their dilemma was in effect that of Indian brahmins who, while resisting the Sanskritization process as a threat to the uniqueness of their prestige, could hardly attack the principles on which it was based except by claiming an essentialist definition of their caste, based wholly on descent. Thus it is with Greek élitists, who claimed special exemption from the taint of Turkish blood in order to maintain the ideological justification of their power.

I have written elsewhere (Herzfeld 1987, 1992) of the way in which Greeks today explain why they still remain imperfect Europeans, by deft allusion to the historical Fall of the City of Constantine in 1453 resulting in cultural contamination analogous to the consequences for humanity at large of original sin. This is a secular cultural theodicy explaining how imperfection may subsist in a world supposedly ordained in the cultural sphere by Pallas Athene much as it is in the moral sphere by the Christian Deity. This argument is derived from Weber's (1963) analysis of theodicy, which, given nation-state claims to transcendence, is surely as applicable to such cultural realizations as it is to religion in the strict sense. That analogy encapsulates the Greeks' painful and prolonged internalization of an orientalism more usefully treated as a practical rather than as a purely textual phenomenon (Herzfeld 1991): just as original sin serves as the explanation of a social world that constantly seems intent on subverting the divine will, so too the taint of oriental culture 'explains' Greece's externally attributed and by now tragically internalized sense of failure to achieve full democracy, civic responsibility, and moderation in all things—those hallmarks of the lost secular paradise that, allegedly in the Enlightenment canon, constituted classical antiquity.

'Practical orientalism/occidentalism' is predicated upon social actors' capacity for evoking prototypes of cultural, heroic, or other exemplary antecedents—this being the focus also of Victor Turner's (1974) 'social drama' at work in the lives of such figures as Thomas à Becket or the Mexican revolutionary leader Zapata, as well as my own 'poetics of social life' (Herzfeld 1985). There are other aspects of the model, however, to which we must pay attention, notably those that situate the particular strategic forms in the context of existing political inequalities. Thus, in a country like Greece, which largely owes its independence to the self-interest of other, stronger nations (Couloumbis, Petropulos, and Psomiades 1976), one will find an especially painful awareness of the inequality of cultural models. In Greece, furthermore, this appears most fully developed in the issue of defining a national language, with the purist version syntactically calqued on foreign prototypes but simultaneously claimed as the restored original of the local tongue. That awareness of inequality may easily take the form of a stereotypical cultural history that social actors evoke quite consciously at any moment when they feel under inspection from abroad—for example, when anthropologists appear on the scene—or when they are engaged in an internal struggle for power and can deploy such evocations in support of their respective claims to moral authority.

In the study of Rethemnos just mentioned, for example, I pointed in the economic sphere to the contrast one frequently encounters between the self-consciously classicizing economic models of the formalistic *aghora* and the equally strongly marked orientalism of the bargaining and sharp practice that more easily comes under the heading of *pazari*. It is a consequence of the brutal tyranny of philologism in Greece that actors know these terms to be themselves respectively classical Greek and Turkish in their immediate derivation. (The Greeks' apparent fascination with etymology is not, as some would have it, a mark of profound devotion to the classical heritage, but a pervasive expression of their unavoidable and sadly consuming preoccupation with meeting an externally imposed cultural standard.) Are the Greeks, they ask, European or Oriental? Why does it matter? For hardly a day goes by in Athens without some daily newspaper asking, with palpable *Angst*, whether Greece belongs to 'the West' or to the 'Third World/Orient'?

'Practical orientalism' thus appears, for example, in the alternating denigration of bargaining as a Turkish way of doing business and the recognition of its familiarity and inevitability in economic relations among people who were each other's intimates and who would thus despise

—and condemn—any attempt to put transactions into a formal, written contract, seeing in such devices the denial of sociability and intimacy. When does one decry bargaining, and when does one embrace it? This is largely a question of audience: before foreigners, bargaining is both demeaning and yet an effective way of playing on their thirst for the picturesque, while their absence makes it the only acceptable mode of economic interaction among close associates. The tactic of appealing to the picturesque reveals the extent to which the national economy is beholden to tourism, with its culturally and economically hegemonic implications. Such cultural embarrassments do indeed seem to necessitate a cultural theodicy, particularly in a nation that is ideologically defined as proud of both its illustrious heritage and, metonymically, its tradition of individualistic devotion to independence.

Note, especially, that the same set of actions may be viewed as either negative or positive. To the extent that such evaluations occur within the logic of practical orientalism, they derive straightforwardly enough from considerations of audience: bargaining is good because it is the hallmark of ordinary social life, bad because foreigners see it and deride it as a failure to live up to those of their cultural standards to which the Greeks have been tied. But what of actions the interpretations of which may oscillate, not between 'negative–oriental' and 'positive–familiar', but between 'oriental' and 'occidental' *tout court*? That is my concern here: with the practical consequences of seeing certain kinds of action and certain categories or styles of marketable commodity as either oriental or occidental.

This approach will help us to make sense of a puzzlement that arises, I suggest, from our own taxonomic imperatives—from the desire, above all, to classify everything as belonging, essentialistically, to one set or the other. (This taxonomic habit is also common among the Greeks themselves, and indeed is one of the most difficult kinds of cultural negotiation to deal with as a visitor: hence my embarrassment at being asked whether the Greeks were Orientals or Europeans. But that is a perfect instance of how we end up blaming the perhaps unwilling recipient of an occidentalizing ideology for its consequences.)

This anti-essentialist approach, which substitutes the clash of interpretations for a formal binarism of essentialized object classes, may help make sense of certain paradoxes of practical occidentalism. For example, the adoption of emblematically 'Western' clothes or other symbols of externally derived status—reproductions of political hegemony built or draped around the consumer's body—does not mean passive acquiescence in the hegemony of this essentialized 'West'. One commonly sees jeans-clad anti-American demonstrators clamouring for revenge against the source of their collective cultural humiliation. To view this phenomenon as a kind of 'cargo cultism' would be, even without the salutary warnings that Lamont Lindstrom offers us in this volume, an extraordinarily condescending act of 'othering'. Greeks have internalized all too successfully a discourse that extols 'the West' in terms that are no less stereotypical, no less condescendingly hegemonic, than the frank orientalism that pervades the pages of travel tales from the fifteenth century to the present.

Stereotypes are both instrument and symbol of hegemony, as they flood the hidden corners of everyday awareness. Like a barium enema, they brightly outline the cultural indigestion of which the national patient so bitterly complains. It is in this sense that I suggest as a parallel and complement to 'practical orientalism' the equally grounded phenomenon of 'practical occidentalism'. We must look, not only at the discourse of European identity that so pervades the Greek national media, but also at its less verbally explicit but equally pragmatic reception in the consumerist world that is so central to Greece today. For if some self-appointed critics from the 'West' today decry the consumerism they see in the streets of Athens (or, more horrifically yet, of the villages), their stance is just the latest in a series of attacks designed to castigate the Greeks for living up to the standard so arbitrarily imposed on them from outside. These attacks keep the Greeks in their appointed place on the margins of Europe, even while imposing an economic regime under which it is hard to imagine the Greeks being able to do otherwise.

The purchasing of goods clearly marked as 'Western'—whether 'European' or 'American'—represents a striving for cultural purity that conflicts with indigenous concepts of intimacy and everyday-ness (*kathimerinotita*). 'Western' control is achieved in two, mutually contrasted ways: either through high prices with their implications of scarcity value, or by flooding the market (although the latter, as we shall see, is more commonly associated with the supposedly 'oriental' cultural profile of mass production). These intrusions of assertively 'Western' culture are also 'tamed' by being brought into a definition of 'tradition' which, while seeming to co-opt them, is actually co-opted *by* them. As a result, a whole range of relatively expensive goods and techniques is newly classified as 'traditional'. Practical occidentalism entails detaching the category of the 'traditional' from the formulaic sense of 'backward, therefore oriental', and conflating it with being 'tasteful, therefore Western'—a move that is further complicated by the increasingly unchallenged assumption that anything 'traditional' must be 'classical', and therefore 'Greek'—which automatically, by a different route, similarly makes it 'Western'. The circle has closed around the definition of 'tradition', thus realizing the nationalist and neo-classical dream of redefining everything European as quintessentially Greek. Occidentalism in Greece is thus not merely imitative, as the orientalist thesis would have it. It is an active attempt by significant segments of the Greek intelligentsia and political leadership to *reclaim* what a mischievously literal reading of the West's propaganda now allows Greeks to consider 'their own' (see Herzfeld 1987: 21). If the adoption of French syntactic structures in *katharevousa* presaged this process, the invasion of blue jeans combines with new exaltations of 'folk art' to inform a new sense of cultural independence and reclamation precisely in those zones of everyday action where outsiders see only crass imitation and consumerism.

Values of Western individualism

One of the paradoxes of modern Greek identity lies in the common circumstance that the 'individualism' and 'independence' or 'love of freedom' that supposedly characterize the Greeks' European essence, and that (in the ideological language of pre-1989 *realpolitik*) set the Greeks categorically in contrast with their communist neighbours, can also be seen as unruly lawlessness and primitive atomism.[3] This sense of inner contradiction reaches an extreme of intensity with the conundrum my sheep-stealing friends in the mountains of west-central Crete pose for the authorities: as 'thieves' (*kleftes*), they both claim commonality with the guerrillas (*kleftes*) who have been canonized as the backbone of the anti-Turkish resistance in the nineteenth century and at the same time violate the provisions and spirit of the law. If they are persecuted, they can deploy the same symbolic logic, accusing the authorities of being latter-day Turks and thus hoisting them by their own, self-occidentalizing petard.[4]

Some may protest that Cretan sheep-thieves are not typical of the country today, if indeed they ever were. This is true enough; but what does it really mean? The example I have just given is extreme in the degree to which it shows the authorities, bearers of an official ideology, confronted by a practical dilemma. The issue, however, goes far beyond the activities of a few thousand sheep-thieves in the Cretan mountains. It takes its most common and most recognizable form in the ambivalence with which most Greeks react to the concept of *eghoismos* or 'self-regard'.

Ever since Campbell (1964) pointed to its centrality in the lives of the northern Greek, transhumant Sarakatsani, among whom it is indeed a particular object of theodicy since it is seen as an endemic and inevitable feature of social life that conflicts with Christian ideals of harmony and humility, this concept has been recognized as both a driving force (positive) and a disruptive drag on development (negative). More specifically, as I first learned from the sheep-thieves of Glendi, it can take the form of both the sense of economic competition that drives a villager to open a coffee house because his neighbour has already done so (positive) and the jealousy that leads him to attack that same neighbour and destroy his property as well as his reputation (negative). The positive kind of *eghoismos* can be adumbrated to the occidentalist model of Greek national character, in that it signals—and enables—the kind of folk Thatcherism that has always been the ideological goal of conservative, pro-Western Greek cultural theorists.[5] The negative variety, by direct contrast, represents the divisiveness that springs, allegedly, from 'Turkish' elements in the Greek national character. While these evaluations of *eghoismos* exhibit a fair degree of variation across Greek communities (Herzfeld 1980), their relationship to the values of self-concealment and self-display shows how easily *eghoismos* can become part of the cultural debate. Is the term to be seen as atomism (negative and disruptive) or as individualism (positive and an ethical source of national independence)? In each case the same local concept is at stake, its coherence marked by the consistent use of the single Greek term, its fracturing into complementary orientalist and occidentalist images the consequence of a treacherous and intrusive ideology that leads Greeks to judge themselves by the standards of outsiders.

Today, understandably, political leaders would not eagerly use the term *eghoismos* to describe the incentive-based economism that legitimizes its positive realization. Indeed, they decry the selfishness that causes businesses to fracture so easily—a tendency that does in fact seem to be based in Crete on the instability of kinship-based alliances subject to the centrifugal competition of siblings' households. In Rethemnos, business operations set up by brothers are rarely much more stable than the rare (and usually short-lived) extended households, and for much the same reasons. Arguing that their wives' and children's interests bring them into an unseemly conflict that threatens the ideological amity of the sibling group, and hence (which in Crete is a serious consideration) of the larger agnatic group that it represents, men find such co-operation hard to sustain. This negative evaluation of instability, however, also translates into a positive version in two ways: on the siblings' side it shows that the brothers will sacrifice even economic advancement to the virtues of sibling solidarity, while in the business world it signals the importance of removing all business activities from the realm of kinship and marks the emergence of professionalism as an ethical and social construct. It also weakens the locally based co-operative movement that was so assiduously fostered by the socialist governments of 1981–9, inasmuch as the latter often brought close agnatic kin into just such unstable economic relationships.

For all these reasons, then, economic Thatcherites in Greece could find in these social phenomena the grounds for their blunt Social Darwinism. Arguing within the larger framework of the privatization programme espoused by the ruling (and conservative) New Democracy party, they could argue that co-operatives would not work because they were against human nature—thereby, very significantly, conflating the *eghoismos* of the culturally corrupted Greeks with the generic baseness of post-edenic human nature.[6]

The answer, say these conservatives, is to bring competition out of its embedded and sometimes destructive role in personal relationships and into active play as an organized feature of economic life. Here they point to the very same phenomena that they elsewhere decry as evidence of the Greeks' inability to co-operate, in order to claim that the Greek national character is conducive to productive competition. During the summer of 1992, at the opening ceremonies for the annual Cretan handicrafts exhibition in Rethemnos mounted by EOMMEX (the National Organization for Small and Medium-Sized Businesses and Handicrafts), several speakers—including a former and present government minister with strong family connections to the pastoral communities of the highlands who is a powerful voice in the ruling New Democracy party—extolled the virtues of small-scale business productivity and its essentially competitive character, and linked the latter both politically and culturally with Greece's (highly controversial) absorption by the post-Maastricht European Community. EOMMEX seeks to encourage the development of such small-scale business ventures, as the means not only of fostering competitive values at home, but also of driving the mass-produced goods of Japan and Taiwan out of the local market. One could easily, and I think justifiably, read into these speeches the twin arguments that the Greeks are 'natural' capitalists and that the mass-produced goods from the orient represent the de-individualization that typifies oriental cultures.[7] What gives this reading some weight is the extent to which all the speakers at the exhibition opening sought to link the capitalist competitiveness they were openly promoting with the *kind* of goods that the EOMMEX-supported

THE WAITING

IT IS DARK, AND I AM WARM AND FORMLESS, FLOATING.

by Summer Cowley

enterprises were producing—mostly the products of small cottage industries that might indeed be expected to serve as flashpoints of local competition (pottery, embroideries, carved wood). These goods are all
self-consciously presented as 'traditional'.

The production of tradition

Not all 'tradition' is necessarily 'invented' (*pace*, perhaps, Hobsbawm and
Ranger 1983), and questions as to whether it is 'genuine or spurious'
(Handler and Linnekin 1984) must always be read in an ironic sense. The
binarism of traditional and modern that one encounters in Greece, however, is clearly and unambiguously a proxy opposition, standing in for the
clash of values between orientalists and occidentalists. It is also, as I have
repeatedly emphasized,[8] an instrument of power, always implying a hierarchical relationship between any two categories, and always subject to
whatever measure of negotiation may be possible under existing political
conditions.

Much less clear, however, is how to align these symbolic pairs with
each other. It is my contention that to subject them to the discipline of a
structuralist 'two-column diagram' (in the idiom of Needham 1973, etc.)
is to miss the point, which is that the very concept of tradition—marked
as a positive virtue—is the object of serious contestation between those
who wish to claim it for a sort of nativist self-orientalizing (the 'Romeic'
ideologues who celebrate the Byzantine Turkish and Arabic as well as the
folk elements of Greek culture) and those who wish to include it in an
essentializing proof of Greece's impeccable occidentality (the 'Hellenists'
or 'neo-classicists'). Thus, the way in which 'tradition' is adduced in
these debates, and above all in the EOMMEX exhibition speeches (all by
party loyalists of New Democracy), may have little to do with what is
actually produced under that label. It is rather much more a question of
how the labels index larger ideological formations. Hoteliers may proudly
point to their furnishings as 'traditionally Cretan' (and indeed in this they
are following however unconsciously the recommendations of at least one
commission on the historic reconstruction of the Old Town of Rethemnos[9]).
A restaurateur may insist that his food is 'pure'—he uses olive oil rather
than the infidel import of corn oil, for example, and note again the
symbolism of purity—and therefore traditional. A householder may in-
sert a hearth of unmistakably Western European design into his house
plan as the mark of his adherence to traditional values (see Herzfeld 1991:
230–2). But these are all acts of attribution. Far from representing the

essential qualities of classes of objects they strategically essentialize particular objects or designs as possessing the intrinsic qualities that define the indefinable: 'tradition'. Attempts to list the particular traits of traditional design to the contrary, the rhetoric of traditionalism marks the site of Greek debates about occident and orient. One form of essentialism, that of 'tradition' reified and infinitely reproduced, marks the contestation of another—the question of whether that tradition is 'really' Eastern or Western.

This incorporation of tradition into the occidentalizing mode occurs in official discourse. It emerges, for example, from the attempts made by the national Archaeological Service to compromise with the local population over their conservation efforts in Rethemnos. Faced with the residents' implacable hostility to each and every attempt to define the Old Town of Rethemnos as a 'monument' (*mnimio*), a term that significantly evokes the nationalist folklorists' (e.g. Politis 1909; see Herzfeld 1982) preoccupation with 'monuments of the word', the conservators sought instead to bring the Old Town under the more relaxed regime of 'traditional neighbourhoods' (*paradhosiakes sinikies*). This device was largely unsuccessful, however, because the mere suggestion that tradition would be subject to bureaucratic regulation placed it outside the residents' conception of what constituted their familiar and socially significant surroundings.

It was clearly an occidentalizing discourse. We should not be led astray by the fact that it entailed the preservation of Turkish as well as Venetian remnants, despite the fulminations of those residents who turned the official discourse against itself by demanding the demolition of all *tourkospita* (literally, 'Turk-houses').[10] As I noted in the earlier study (Herzfeld 1991), the simple fact that architecture was preserved fitted the liberal ideology of self-occidentalization: we are not like the Turks, the (historically untenable) argument goes, who destroy our churches and turn them into mosques or museums. (Those who opposed the preservation of the older houses, however, aligned their denunciations of the 'unclean' Turkish buildings with a savage attack on what they chose to portray as the anti-business left wing and rejected the equation of the picturesque with the quintessentially Greek and European.) I would add to that the observation now that this stance of cultural tolerance also harmonized well with that aspect of folk social theory according to which a Turk should be treated with even greater hospitality than one would show a fellow-Greek, since this demonstrates the host's—and his culture's—moral as well as cultural superiority. Once again, we see that the pedantic attribution of essentializing traits to the *realia* of cultural contest completely misses the point; the issue is that of what these discursive tactics are *for*.

Technique and product: or, how tradition emerges from modernity

The concept of 'tradition' does not, then, simply reproduce an image of Ottoman times, nor is it necessarily associated with concomitant images of 'backwardness'. On the contrary, it may be the very hallmark of modernity. A parquet-floor-maker explained to me that he was interested in the latest techniques of wood preparation and patterning, and expressed impatience with the un-artisan-like haste and slovenliness with which, he asserted, Greek customers were prepared to see their floors constructed. His techniques, which require prefabricated wooden strips made to an international standard, announce an eminently 'Western' identity, and constitute an element of the pursuit of occidental elegance that so characterizes the production of habitation spaces in Greece today. Yet his discourse continually brought his work back into the realm of 'tradition'. To find out more about carpentry on Crete, he sent me on to a 'traditional' woodcarver (whose bookends with a crude copy of Eleftherios Venizelos's face typified another recent construction of 'tradition' on Crete[11]); he claimed to want to retire so he could devote himself, as his elderly father was currently doing, to the fashioning of 'traditional' utensils and implements (for which he had plausibly old and rustic models in his workshop); and he particularly delighted in my interest in his work: it showed, he argued, that, *because* his craft was on the wane, it must indeed be traditional in its own right.

Prominent in his discourse is the combination of ideas about technique that were demonstrably of Western European industrial origin with the nostalgic evocation of artisanship and the unceasing lament for its lost virtues. This combination clearly articulated an understanding of 'tradition' that would horrify a museological purist but would presumably delight the Thatcherites of the handicrafts exhibit. This focus on a kind of *activity* deflects attention away from the physical appearance of the *product* and provides a justification for regarding as traditional objects that from a strictly aesthetic perspective would not easily gain admittance to that category. Thus making activity rather than aesthetics the object of the discourse permits actors to reframe the description of the product in a manner that disguises potential contradictions. Here in a brief vignette lies perhaps the most distinctive characteristic of occidentalism in Greece. For it is an occidentalism that must constantly strive to wean 'tradition' away from the orientalizing opposite pole. This cultural alchemy is a kind of practical essentialism: it relies on representing the activity (or process) as intrinsic to the product.

Foreign visitors to Greece, carrying their own baggage of nostalgia, see as hideous intrusions of modern industrial culture the very things that delight the bourgeois sense of occidental order there, and cannot easily understand how these become adumbrated to 'tradition'. For the foreigner, representative and (it may be) repository of the ideology that condemns Greece to cultural marginality, the idea that tradition can contain the most obvious *realia* of modernity is simply incomprehensible; and Americans' or West Europeans' horror at the *embourgeoisement* of Greek culture is simply one more round in that favourite Western game (or plot, in the Greek narrative) of forcing the Greeks to play by occidental rules and then chastising them for not noticing that those wily occidentals have gone and changed the rules on them.[12] I am not, of course, arguing that any Greek would see the anti-American protester's blue jeans as 'traditional'. But in a cultural space where parquet floors, wood carvings of modern politicians, and brick-and-brass fireplaces can be seen as traditionally Greek, we should hardly be surprised that what to us seem to be signs of inconsistency—or even ingratitude—should strike Greek observers as entirely appropriate.

For occidentalizing Greeks, a cultural continuum links the traditional with the modern, a necessary step on the return road to cultural Eden, and places *both* in opposition to the evil intrusiveness, the un-Greek impurity, represented by the infidel Turks and their influence. For those Greeks who have not yet unlearned the imposed lessons of Enlightenment Hellenism, 'the West' *is* the Greek tradition. The logic is exactly that whereby, two centuries ago, puristic linguists imported French and German syntactical structures into their so-called 'pure' Greek language, and whereby bourgeois townsfolk imitated—and bourgeois villagers now imitate—the canons of West European architectural style, once neoclassical and today starkly modernist, in preference to other models that too strongly recall the East. If the artisans whose job it is to preserve and rebuild tradition say it is traditional, then traditional it is.

Thus it is that today, throughout the length and breadth of Greece, one is confronted by a ritualistic succession of occicentalizing motifs, encapsulated in a rhetoric of tradition. Weber, surveying this disenchanted scene, might well have noted that these motifs represented the deadening routinization of 'the West' at the hands of a conformist bourgeoisie. It is their very replication that effectively suffocates any challenge to their cultural authority. Indeed, if nationalism is at least analogous to religion (Kapferer 1988; Herzfeld 1992), these recurrent icons of occidentalism represent not so much a cargo cult of immediate redemption, as a persuasively Christian yearning for the return to Eden. Renée Hirschon (1989) has pointed out that the everyday world of *soi-disant* atheist communists among the Asia Minor refugee population of Piraeus is suffused with the symbols of Orthodoxy. Why, then, should we be in the slightest degree surprised to find that the cultural idiom of *soi-disant* traditionalists in the same country should continue to operate within the parameters of a theodicy that through nearly two millenniums of Christianity has offered a singularly comprehensive pragmatic absolution from sins venal, legal, and cultural?

Acknowledgements

While the present topic was not the object of my research in the summer of 1992, some of the data are derived from work on apprenticeship that I conducted with a Small Grant from the Spencer Foundation. Earlier research was conducted with the help of a Fellowship for Study and Research from the National Endowment for the Humanities. Neither funding agency is in any way responsible for the contents of this chapter or of any other product of the research thus conducted.

Notes

1 The form *Rethemnos* (n.) is local. 'Rethymnon' is the neo-classical spelling used in English-language transliterations. Under the Venetians the town was called Rettimo; under the Turks, it became Resime.
2 This may seem an extraordinary statement. Readers should bear in mind, however, that Greece is perhaps the only country of which the prefix 'modern' is required to distinguish it—often in a pejorative sense—from its ancient forebears. The literature on this topic is enormous; see especially William St Clair (1972) for an account of contemporary impatience with what was seen as the predominant oriental element in (modern) Greek culture on the part of those who claimed most enthusiastically to be saving the country from the infidel and uncultured Turks.
3 This conceit appears in the mid-19th cent. in pro-Greek writings (see Herzfeld 1982: 59–60), while the *zadruga* has long served as an ideological demonstration of endemic Slavic communalism. Such stereotypes play an important role in the construction of European identity; see also Nadel-Klein (this volume).
4 Thus, e.g. sheep-thieves in highland Crete may show signs of treating the Athens government in this way (Herzfeld 1985: 19), much as Capodistrias, who served as the first President of Greece (1828–31), defined the Peloponnesian

landowners who resisted central power in the newly independent Greek state as 'Christian Turks' (Dakin 1973: 60).

5 The ambiguities of *kleftis* ('thief'/'national hero') and *eghoistis* ('egotist'/ 'individualist') may reflect the cultural tensions that I have elsewhere (Herzfeld 1987: 95–122) labelled 'disemic'—i.e. as semiotically realized as a play of self-presentation and self-knowledge at several nested ('segmentary') collective levels. It may also be relevant that, in Greek, terms of powerful emotion do not have the unambiguous positive/negative marking of English; compare, for example, *kaimos*, 'grief' but also 'enthusiasm'; *lakhtara*, 'longing' but also 'sudden deep fear'; or even *thousiasi* (Cretan dialect), 'enthusiasm' but also 'deep emotional pain' (Herzfeld 1993).

The instability of fraternal co-operation (see Herzfeld 1980; Levy 1956), which parallels the instability of combined landholdings and extended family residential arrangements throughout Greece (and many other parts of the Balkan region), can serve as the embodiment of, alternatively, 'individualism' or 'amoral familism' (Banfield 1958), according to whether the discursive context is an occidentalizing or an orientalizing one.

6 This is a metaphorical link between original sin and the cultural 'taint' of Turkishness (see Herzfeld 1987: p. xxx). I have intentionally suggested through my choice of language here the characteristic conflation of cultural contempt with notions of miscegenation so characteristic both of folk theories and of the dominant rhetoric of state nationalism.

7 This is the logic of what I have elsewhere (Herzfeld 1987) called 'the European ideology', according to which what unites all Europeans is their capacity for cultural and psychological individuation. This is the corollary of the popular view that 'the [oriental] natives all look alike', as, apparently, do their products (which are therefore debarred from the category of 'art').

To my regret I did not record these speeches at the time. The minister's was printed in the local newspapers, to the total exclusion of that given by the head of the local chamber of commerce, a much more minor official. He, poor man, tried to get his text published; not only did the newspaper to which he sent it fail to publish the text until it was no longer newsworthy, but they then unceremoniously threw it away on the grounds that 'manuscripts are not returned'. He had not kept a copy himself. All this suggests that what he had to say was in fact so commonplace as to be infinitely reproducible; and, in fact, he offered a remarkably similar set of comments in the course of an informal interview he gave me at that time.

8 I emphasize this point again here because it is misunderstood with disturbing—if revealing—frequency. Merely by pointing to a binary opposition at the level of ethnographic observation, one risks resuscitating fears of resurgent structuralism. But my point, most fully articulated in Herzfeld (1987), is precisely that we should not ignore such binarisms just because they conflict with our own ideological predilections. On the contrary, they are a reliable indicator of specific ways of reading inequality and indeed of justifying it (see

esp. Carrier's Introduction to this volume for an exemplary case in point), and, as such, should always be the object of close ethnographic and analytical scrutiny—as, by way of a corollary, should the rhetoric of those who persist in representing each and every report of binary categories as a blow for those in power. Much the same can be said of etymology; as Vico (1744) demonstrated, the fact that etymology is usually an instrument of legitimization does not thereby automatically exclude it from the realm of historically informed debunking.

9 See the furniture plans included in the official 1974 plan for the historic reconstruction of Old Rethemnos (Moutsopoulos and Zervas n.d.; see esp. 'suggestions for the furnishing of rooms for rent').

10 There is a considerable—and often vituperative—local literature on this, carried forth in such newspapers as *Rethemniotika Nea*.

11 Venizelos is usually presented as the prototypical case of the Cretan hero who gave all to an ingrate nation. He has become virtually the secular saint of all the political parties with representation on Crete, despite the wide ideological differences among them.

12 The failure of the European Community and the United States to react sympathetically to Greek objections to the use of the name 'Macedonia' by the former Yugoslav republic is another example: occidental politicians are no longer interested in the resuscitation of classical antiquity and no longer have the educational background to make that goal comprehensible or desirable.

References

BANFIELD, EDWARD C. (1958). *The Moral Basis of a Backward Society*. New York: Free Press.

CAMPBELL, J. K. (1964). *Honour, Family, and Patronage: A Study of Institutions and Moral Values in a Greek Mountain Community*. Oxford: Clarendon Press.

COULOUMBIS, T. A., PETROPULOS, JOHN A., and PSOMIADES, H. J. (1976). *Foreign Interference in Greek Politics: An Historical Perspective*. New York: Pella.

DAKIN, DOUGLAS (1973). *The Greek Struggle for Independence, 1821–1833*. London: Batsford.

HANDLER, RICHARD, and LINNEKIN, JOCELYN (1984). 'Tradition, Genuine or Spurious', *Journal of American Folklore*, 97: 273–90.

HERZFELD, MICHAEL (1980). 'Social Tension and Inheritance by Lot in Three Greek Villages', *Anthropological Quarterly*, 53: 91–100.

——(1982). *Ours Once More: Folklore, Ideology, and the Making of Modern Greece*. Austin, Tex.: University of Texas Press.

——(1985). *The Poetics of Manhood: Contest and Identity in a Cretan Mountain Village*. Princeton, NJ: Princeton University Press.

——(1987). *Anthropology through the Looking-Glass: Critical Ethnography in the Margins of Europe*. Cambridge: Cambridge University Press.

——(1991). *A Place in History: Social and Monumental Time in a Cretan Town.* Princeton, NJ: Princeton University Press.

——(1992). *The Social Production of Indifference: Exploring the Symbolic Roots of Western Bureaucracy.* Oxford: Berg.

——(1993). 'In Defiance of Destiny: The Management of Time and Gender at a Cretan Funeral', *American Ethnologist*, 20: 241–55.

HIRSCHON, RENÉE (1989). *Heirs of the Greek Catastrophe: The Social Life of Asia Minor Refugees in Piraeus.* Oxford: Clarendon Press.

HOBSBAWM, ERIC, and RANGER, TERENCE (eds.) (1983). *The Invention of Tradition.* Cambridge: Cambridge University Press.

KAPFERER, BRUCE (1988). *Legends of People, Myths of State.* Washington, DC: Smithsonian Institution Press.

LEVY, HARRY L. (1956). 'Property Distribution by Lot in Present Day Greece', *Transactions of the American Philological Association*, 87: 42–6.

MOUTSOPOULOS, N. C., and ZERVAS, G. D. (n.d.). *Design on [sic] the Protection the Improvement and the Presentation of the Ancient City of Rethymnon: Summary of the Report.* N.p.

MOUZELIS, NICOS P. (1978). *Modern Greece: Facets of Underdevelopment.* London: Macmillan.

NEEDHAM, RODNEY (ed.) (1973). *Right and Left: Essays on Dual Symbolic Classification.* Chicago: University of Chicago Press.

POLITIS, N. G. (1909). 'Laography', *Laografia*, 1: 3–18.

ST CLAIR, WILLIAM (1972). *That Greece Might Still Be Free: The Philhellenes in the War of Independence.* London: Oxford University Press.

SOTIROPOULOS, DIMITRI (1977). 'Diglossia and the National Language Question in Modern Greece', *Linguistics*, 197: 5–31.

TURNER, VICTOR (1974). *Dramas, Fields, and Metaphors.* Ithaca, NY: Cornell University Press.

VICO, GIAMBATTISTA (1744). *Principij di scienza nuova.* (3rd edn.) Naples: Stamperia Muziana.

WEBER, MAX (1963). *The Sociology of Religion*, trans. Ephraim Fischoff. Boston: Beacon Press.

Occidentalism in the East: The Uses of the West in the Politics and Anthropology of South Asia

Jonathan Spencer

> We speak of Eastern and Western culture. But if we analyse this concept against a background of anthropology we shall not be able to find many elements of culture that can be definitely pointed out as peculiar to Western culture and foreign to us.
>
> (Martin Wickremesinghe 1992: 120)

A strong case can be made for treating South Asia as the region in which occidentalism has received its fullest and most frequent expression, both in anthropology and in the wider world of politics and culture. Indeed, there is simply so much talk of 'the West' in India and Sri Lanka that my comments here have to be schematic in the extreme. Nevertheless, the examples I discuss allow me to join together the two major strands running through this volume: the uses of occidentalism in anthropology and other academic writing, and the occidentalism of politicians and other non-academic members of the post-colonial order. But in joining these two strands I also reveal the political and intellectual complexity of the different phenomena which the contributors have glossed as occidentalism. In keeping with the general spirit of the collection, I do this through the discussion of specific examples of occidentalist argument.

I start by looking at anthropological occidentalisms in South Asia, first in order to demonstrate the use of what I call the rhetoric of authenticity—the use of the West as a rhetorical counter which guarantees the anthropologist's real understanding of the non-West; and secondly in order to justify this volume's choice of occidentalism as the master trope under which to subsume other dichotomies such as traditional/modern and rural/urban. I then examine some South Asian uses of occidentalism in the public sphere, where it serves above all as mnemonic for the cultural contradictions engendered by colonial domination. I do this by sketching the positions of three Sri Lankan figures, all nationalist writers from the middle and late colonial period. I also briefly discuss the version of Gandhi's 'affirmative Orientalism' recently presented by the Indian cultural critic Ashis Nandy. These examples allow me to reconstruct something of the political context of different occidentalisms, but in so doing I uncover an unexpected paradox: where anthropological occidentalism tends to efface the colonial encounter, indigenist occidentalism foregrounds it. In the face of this I offer one preliminary conclusion. Not only is essentialism an inevitable and not terribly remarkable feature of our world, as James Carrier points out in his Introduction. But, as the uses of occidentalism are at once various and complex, so simple-minded anti-essentialism is both politically and theoretically inadequate as a response.

The rhetoric of authenticity

Western reason has had a poor time of it in Sri Lanka of late. Its mixed fortunes exemplify the uneasy juxtapositions and entanglements of academic and popular argument which I want to explore, and which up to now have been kept apart in the different chapters of this book. For example, a number of Sri Lankan liberals—organized through groups with titles like the Committee for Rational Development (CRD)—have made frequent appeals to 'rationality' in their attempts to question the historical and political vision of what they see as an oppressive, and often racist, Sinhala nationalism (cf. Tennekoon 1990). There have been two strands to their work: a critique of nationalist historiography, and a positive promotion of federalism and multiculturalism as the basis for a political solution to the ethnic problem.

Each, however, has its problems. The critique of the nationalist interpretation of the past, particularly that part of it based on readings of the Buddhist chronicle the *Mahavamsa*, has been accused of missing the point anthropologically. While welcoming the liberals' efforts in general, Bruce Kapferer suggested that their problem was that, in their analyses, 'the critics argue from positions *outside* the myths and the legends' (Kapferer 1988: 40; my emphasis). The positions in question are those of Western rationality (1988: 41). This 'rationality' is linked to class domination in post-colonial Sri Lanka. It misses the point of the stories from the chronicles, though, because what Kapferer calls the 'myths' have their own logic: 'They have force because they enshrine and incorporate

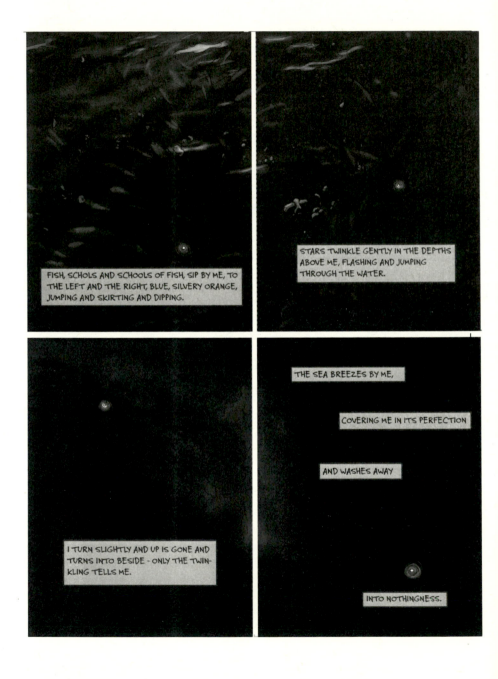

FISH, SCHOLS AND SCHOOLS OF FISH, SIP BY ME, TO THE LEFT AND THE RIGHT, BLUE, SILVERY ORANGE, JUMPING AND SKIRTING AND DIPPING.

STARS TWINKLE GENTLY IN THE DEPTHS ABOVE ME, FLASHING AND JUMPING THROUGH THE WATER.

I TURN SLIGHTLY AND UP IS GONE AND TURNS INTO BESIDE - ONLY THE TWINKLING TELLS ME.

THE SEA BREEZES BY ME,

COVERING ME IN ITS PERFECTION

AND WASHES AWAY

INTO NOTHINGNESS.

a fundamental intentionality, an orientation toward the world of experience, which engages many Sinhalese in their everyday life' (1988: 48).

The appeal to multiculturalism and federalism also has problems. In
the early 1990s the most consistent opposition to multiculturalism came
from a group of militant Sinhala nationalists, led by two well-known
intellectuals, a mathematician and a novelist, Nalin de Silva and Gunadasa
Amarasekera, and supported most conspicuously by students, especially
science students from the University of Colombo. The group is known as
Jathika Chintanaya, which roughly translates as 'national world-view,
style of knowledge, or way of life'.[1] It opposes what it describes as the
'Western' or 'Judaic Chintanaya'. In a newspaper interview in 1991, de
Silva explained the difference between the 'Jathika' and the 'Western'
Chintanaya in terms of a contrast between the analytic and the holistic.
'Rationalism' was a vice of the analytic West:

The Western Chintanaya is tied to extreme rationalism. But we do not have even
a term (an equivalent) in Sinhala for rationalism. Instead we believe in 'Cause and
Effect'. If we are to follow rationalism, which is a very dangerous thing then you
can even kill your father and rationalise it. Get me anything—I will rationalise it.

He then went on to decry multiculturalism and multi-ethnicity as 'a
brainchild of the Judaic Chintanaya that paves the way for a "divide and
rule" policy' (*Island* 1991).[2]

This juxtaposition illustrates two points. One is the pervasiveness of
the East–West opposition in the politics of culture in South Asia. The
other is the diversity of uses to which that opposition may be put. Both
Kapferer and de Silva are employing images of the West as part of a
rhetoric of authenticity, a claim to escape the prison of 'Western rationality' in order to penetrate to some deeper, more authentic understanding
of 'the Sinhalese'. Kapferer's argument is framed within a broad contrast
between hierarchical and egalitarian ontologies of nationalism, realized in
the political cultures of Sri Lanka and Australia, and which effortlessly
maps onto the equally broad contrast between East and West.[3] The
leaders of Jathika Chintanaya also employ broad East–West contrasts in
their arguments. But this is not to claim that the same political consequences necessarily follow from the use of the same rhetorical strategy:
Kapferer makes clear his sympathy with the very proponents of multiculturalism that de Silva is attacking, and his warning about the limited
effectiveness of empiricist criticism of nationalist ideology is, in practice,
a valid one. Meanwhile the leaders of Jathika Chintanaya have since
moved on from intellectual critique to fervent espousal of a 'military

solution' to the problems of the country's Tamil minority. Later in this chapter, I return to the problem of misreading similar political consequences from formal similarities in rhetoric, and suggest instead we pay more attention to the differing political uses of different, contextually defined occidentalisms.

The problems of an Indian sociology

First, though, I want to start with anthropological talk of the West, and the use of selective images of the West as a device to legitimize differing interpretations of South Asian society. Two of the most important bodies of work in the modern anthropology of South Asia—Louis Dumont's hierarchical theory of Hindu society and McKim Marriott's ethnosociology —both base themselves on distinctive versions of the rhetoric of authenticity. Both Dumont and Marriott have rejected criticisms of their work on the grounds that the critics are too far in thrall to Western assumptions about society and the person. The irony is that the style of argument that Dumont used to see off his own ethnocentric critics in the early 1960s was employed against him by Marriott a decade later: despite appearances to the contrary, Dumont himself was allegedly trapped in Western philosophical and sociological categories which were inappropriate in understanding Indian realities. Yet, for all the similarities in argument, there are important differences between the kinds of occidentalism employed by Dumont and Marriott, and these differences point to two linked but distinct genealogies in anthropological occidentalism, which I shall call positivist and romantic occidentalism. My formulation owes much to George Stocking's delineation of 'scientific' and 'romantic' strains in the anthropological sensibility (Stocking 1988), and something to Johannes Fabian's critique of 'allochronism' (Fabian 1983), although neither is responsible for the unnuanced way in which I develop the argument here.

In this case, the lineage of positivist occidentalism can be traced from Dumont to his teacher Mauss, and thence back to those nineteenth-century evolutionary theories which reconciled the scientific demand for unity with the apparent reality of human difference by placing differences in the present at different points along a temporal scale. I call this 'positivist' rather than, say, 'evolutionary' because its distinctive feature is not necessarily evolutionism, so much as the assumption that East–West distinctions can be reconciled within some more encompassing intellectual framework: that, in the words of one of anthropology's charter texts, 'if law is anywhere it is everywhere' (Tylor in Lévi-Strauss 1969: p. xxi). My choice of 'positivist' rather than 'scientific', indicates the origins of this approach in Comte's positive sociology, and Lévi-Strauss's quotation from Tylor reminds us that universal law was as real a concern for structuralism as it had been for evolutionism.

Romantic occidentalism acknowledges differences in the present without relocating them so explicitly along a temporal scale, but then finds itself constantly threatened by accusations of relativism and cultural solipsism. Romantic occidentalism can be found in the cultural anthropology of David Schneider and, to a lesser extent, Clifford Geertz and its genealogy extends back through Benedict and Mead to Boas and thence to its German roots in Herder and von Humboldt. In the romantic version, cultures exist in parallel, equal but usually very different; in the positivist version, all cultural differences at one level can be subsumed under general laws operating at a more universal level. Weber's comparative sociology draws on both styles of occidentalism, as do its intellectually impoverished successors in modernization theory and the various theories of development that have taken its place. Victorian evolutionism may seem best to exemplify positivist occidentalism, but its presuppositions resurface in all comparisons which position human differences along a single, unitary temporal scale: Pierre Bourdieu's employment of traditional/modern dichotomies, as described by Reed-Danahay in this volume, is but one of many recent social-theoretical examples of the conflation of spatial and temporal differences into the great divide between modern and pre-modern or Western and non-Western. And, as Nadel-Klein shows, other powerful dichotomies like rural and urban, *Gesellschaft* and *Gemeinschaft*, combine the twin axes of time and space: the West is usually the modern urban West. And ironically enough, even talk of the post-modern and the decline of metanarratives inescapably posits a simple three-stage (pre-, modern, post-) metanarrative whose crudeness and implicit universality would warm the hearts of many a Victorian social theorist.

Kapferer positions his interpretation of Sinhala nationalism firmly (but neither uncritically nor uncreatively) within the terms of Dumont's account of South Asia. Dumont is a particularly interesting case because the structure of his intellectual career recapitulates so many of the themes of this volume: an early monograph on the folklore of rural ('traditional', 'pre-modern') France, field-work in India followed by his major synthetic account of Indian society *Homo Hierarchicus*, and now nearly three decades of work tracing the origins of 'our' social assumptions, origins which he finds best exemplified in intellectual history (cf. Galey 1991). While

Dumont's view of India combines élite textual interpretations with ethnographic report, his version of the West, like that of some other anthropologists, depends entirely on the writings of intellectuals, rather than, say, material from the work of social historians. If nothing else, this suggests a somewhat unreflexive attitude to 'our' ideas and 'our' social position. As with Dumont, Marriott's West, even more than his East, values the 'bookview' over the 'fieldview': a point made again and again in Carrier's original critique of anthropological occidentalism (Carrier 1992; cf. Béteille 1990: 490).[4] It is true, however, that in his most recent formulation Marriott acknowledges a potential difference between the academic West and popular thought (Marriott 1990*b*: 2), without displaying a great deal of curiosity about the possible scale and importance of such a difference.

Dumont's comparison of India and the West can be read in two ways. One, exemplified in Mary Douglas's introduction to the first British paperback edition of *Homo Hierarchicus*, stresses India's role as a 'mirror-image': 'a society founded on principles exactly antithetical to those we honour' (Douglas 1972: 12). This (which is more or less Carrier's reading in the Introduction to this volume) would seem to imply a radical gulf between 'us' and 'them'. But Dumont's intention is somewhat subtler than that: for him, India and the West represent not two incommensurable systems dominated by different values, but two extreme positions on a universal continuum. In one, hierarchy dominates and equality is barely acknowledged; in the other—'us', the West—equality reigns supreme. Our problem is not the absence of hierarchy, but our intellectual inability to acknowledge its inevitable presence in social life.[5] For a writer like Dumont, the relationship between West and non-West is not necessarily, as Lindstrom points out in his chapter, as fixed and impermeable as Said's original model may have suggested.

One source of the different interpretations is Dumont's employment of the rhetoric of authenticity in support of what, in the last analysis, he intends as a universalizing theory. From the start, Dumont's important argument for the need to attend to Indian values in understanding Indian society was taken by his critics as evidence of a descent from sociology or anthropology proper to 'culturology'. Indeed, F. G. Bailey's claim in an early exchange with Dumont (which owes much to Radcliffe-Brown's hostility to the 'vague abstraction' called culture), that in certain cases 'a valid sociological understanding' is possible by 'making abstractions immediately from behaviour', with no reference to the ideas of the people concerned, can remind us of just how much anthropology owes to

Dumont's example (Bailey 1959: 90). Nevertheless, Dumont's version of Indian values was on the one hand always selective, while on the other hand he reserved the right to 'add the necessary but implicit links to the principles that the people themselves give' (Dumont and Pocock 1957: 12).

However selective its basis, his interpretation of Indian society was accompanied by a strong version of the rhetoric of authenticity. For example: 'The reader may, of course, refuse to leave the shelter of his own values: he may lay it down that for him man begins with the Declaration of the Rights of Man, and condemn outright anything which departs from it' (Dumont 1980: 2). The home of such timid potential readers is rarely simply 'the West'; more often it is 'the modern West':

There remain the societies of the modern Western type, which go so far as to inscribe the principle of equality in their constitutions. It is indeed true that, if values and not behaviour alone are considered, a profound gap has to be acknowledged between the two kinds. What has happened? Is it possible to take a simple view of it? The societies of the past, most societies, have believed themselves to be based in the order of things, natural as well as social . . . Modern society wants to be 'rational', to break away from nature in order to set up an autonomous human order. (1980: 261)

The talk of 'societies of the past', and the easy transition from space ('Western') to time ('modern'), reminds us of Dumont's debt to his teacher Mauss. Indeed, the totality of Dumont's work, including both the exposition of Indian denials of individuality and equality and the subsequent tracing of the origins of these values of 'ours' in intellectual history, can be seen as a working out on the grand scale of the project sketched so enigmatically in Mauss's late essay on the idea of the person (Mauss 1985). Like Mauss's essay on *The Gift* (1990) (discussed by Carrier in this volume) the essay on the person combines historical and ethnographic material in order to compose a more or less unitary genealogy of 'our' world and its values. In *The Gift* the ethnographic present was combined with material from 'our' past in order to criticize the modern social order; in the essay on the person, written a decade and a half later—and in a darker political climate—'our' central values look altogether more fragile and in need of defence. Both essays retain an evolutionary unity.

As Mauss's essay is as much concerned with continuities as it is with differences, so it is that the distinction between 'gift societies' and 'commodity societies' which Carrier criticizes is better attributed to more recent writers like C. A. Gregory and Marilyn Strathern (cf. Carrier 1992: 208 n. 15). What is interesting is why these recent writers have sought to deny the unity asserted by earlier theorists. This unity of positivist occidentalism is temporal—and what may appear incommensurable differences between 'us' and 'them' in the present are made manageable by assigning 'their' present to a position in 'our' past. As Lindstrom puts it, 'they' are the 'younger brother who struggles behind'. Similarly, when 'they' appear in the wrong place—the geographical West—they are quickly assigned to an earlier time, as Nadel-Klein shows. And in this, talk of the West is above all a way of talking about the modern.

For three decades McKim Marriott has been Dumont's most persistent American critic in the anthropology of South Asia.[6] Since the early 1970s he has argued for what he calls an 'ethnosociology' of South Asian social forms, based not on Western folk sociology, but on properly South Asian assumptions. For Marriott, 'South Asian thought' is essentially monistic, whereas Dumont's arguments about 'purity' and 'pollution', 'status and 'power', 'encompassing' and 'encompassed' reproduce the assumptions of 'dualistic thought in the Judaeo-Christian West' (Marriott and Inden 1977: 231). And Dumont's argument, that India and the modern West present extreme variations on a limited set of ideological possibilities, is dismissed as an a priori assumption (1977: 229). More recently, Marriott has contrasted his efforts with what he rather dismissively characterizes as 'the narrower model of Indian society constructed with some Western categories by Louis Dumont' (Marriott 1990a: p. xiii). And Dumont is one obvious target in the following list of symptoms of Western intellectual colonialism:

Whether aware or not, however, the investigator who seeks ways of asking in rural India about equivalents of Western 'individuals', 'social structures', 'kinship', 'classes', 'statuses', 'rules', 'oppositions', 'solidarities', 'hierarchies', 'authority', 'values', 'ideology', 'religion', 'purity', etc., risks imposing an alien epistemology on those who attempt to answer. (Marriott 1990b: 2)

The ambition of Marriott's ethnosociology is not simply to employ 'indigenous cognitive terms' to build up a cultural model of Indian society (Marriott and Inden 1977: 236), nor to employ those terms in contrastive opposition to the limited assumptions of the 'Western ethnosocial sciences'. The aim now appears to be to work up a systematized version of South Asian social thought which 'may provide better bases for the future claim of an expanded, multicultural set of sciences to have that "universal significance and value" which Weber in 1904 . . . prematurely reserved for rational social thought in the West' (Marriott 1990b: 3)—a kind of rainbow epistemology.

Marriott's programme clearly has precursors and successors in anthropology. The empirical concern with 'codes', 'substances', and 'persons' owes much to the distinctly un-Indian figure of Schneider, while the strong rhetoric of authenticity finds echoes in the recent Melanesian work of Strathern. The very term 'dividual' (discussed by Carrier in his comments on Strathern) is taken from Marriott, while one recent commentator claims that Marriott's version of South Asian social thought 'looks more Melanesian than, say, Chinese' (Appadurai 1988: 755; cf. Marriott and Inden 1977: 227; Strathern 1988: 348–9 n. 7). There is no doubt that, like Dumont's earlier argument for the need to attend to indigenous ideology, Marriott's rhetoric of authenticity—involving the curious figure of a professor from the University of Chicago claiming to speak (in English) the language of a radically non-Western social science—has nevertheless been a salutary influence in forcing ethnographers to listen far more carefully to what people are saying and to attend to the assumptions upon which they are saying it. The same can be said for Dumont. Had Bailey's version of the 'sociology of India' carried the day in the early 1960s, the ethnographic record would have been painfully impoverished. My purpose here is not to challenge the genuine gains in understanding that both Dumont and Marriott have precipitated, but to query the rhetoric of authenticity with which they have felt it necessary to present their arguments.

Marriott's ethnosociology is a particularly striking example of romantic occidentalism in anthropology. Like the romantic version of cultural difference which Boas inherited from Herder and von Humboldt, it is predicated on a vision of bounded, internally homogeneous cultures, in which differences between cultures hover on the edge of an absolute incommensurability, and anthropologists seek out essences, cores, or central cultural symbols. It differs from Dumont's positivist occidentalism in two ways. It makes no attempt to subsume differences in the present under an evolutionary framework in which 'their' present can be discerned in 'our' past. And it attempts, not entirely successfully, to avoid the trap of employing Indian difference as another way of really talking about ourselves. The limited success is evident in the frequency of Marriott's recourse to talk of the West and the Western; a confident ethnosociology would, presumably, be able to turn its back entirely on this sort of contrastive rhetoric.

'A principle feature of orientalist discourse', Lindstrom reminds us, 'is that this promises to describe the other but, in fact, delivers only more stories about the self.' This is only true up to a point: we need to avoid the reductionist argument that any use of contrastive comparison—whether with the West, America, Europe, Euro-Americans, or simply 'us'—means that the writer in question is 'really' writing solely about us and nothing else. This kind of argument itself involves an essentialism of a sort: all we need to know of Bourdieu or Mauss (or Dumont or Marriott) is that they were guilty of the use of essentialized contrasts of us and them. From here it is a short step to the use of essentialism as an excuse for not reading anything written before, say, 1980. At this stage, some would argue, the whole enterprise of anthropological comparison appears imperilled, just as the history of the discipline is suddenly drastically truncated.

It takes little critical acumen to recognize that both Dumont and Marriott do tell us rather a lot about India, despite their frequent use of contrasts with a stereotypical West. Not the least of their importance in this context is the fact that both have thought long and hard about the possibilities and purposes of anthropological comparison. Nevertheless, the structure of occidentalist feeling serves as a filter in their work: just as the version of the West is partial, so too is the contrasted image of India. Like Carrier's description of the Melanesia of the ethnographers, anything apparently occidental, and thus inauthentic, is ignored, leaving the focus firmly on what is taken to be authentically oriental. What is necessarily effaced in this is the shared history that serves as the primary condition of anthropological possibility: the colonial encounter. To mention this is not to deny the need for a comparative anthropology. Cultural differences are not eliminated by reference to shared history, and anthropological comparison can proceed quite satisfactorily without recourse to gross totalizing contrasts between us and them, West and East, as the contributions to this book make amply clear.

To return to that shared history: André Béteille points out that the stereotypical contrast of India and the West, as *homo hierarchicus* and *homo aequalis*, above all denies the history of colonial rule, which can be interpreted as a systematic political and ideological construction built on a premiss of natural inequality (Béteille 1983: 35). Similarly, Marriott's (and Schneider's) claim that code and substance, actor and act, are essentially separate in the West makes little sense in the light of systematic racism, an ideology in which moral differences are embodied in differences of natural substance (Béteille 1990: 498–500). And, however ethnosociologically inauthentic such talk may be, for many Indians today, class is as potentially important as any other source of cultural difference (Kumar 1992: 5).

These points can be linked in many ways to the modern politics of identity in South Asia. Take race, class, and colonialism, for example: in Sri Lanka in the nineteenth century, élite Sinhala intellectuals seized on the colonial discourse of race in order to redefine their own—'Aryan'—position in the scheme of things; as a result, Tamil–Sinhala differences are today described as 'racial' differences in an interpretation of the national past which owes much to colonial ethnology (Rogers 1990; Kemper 1991). In South India, the Aryan–Dravidian just-so story, in which Indian differences were explained as the product of a long historical process in which fair-skinned northern Aryans invaded a continent inhabited by dark-skinned Dravidians, bringing with them various kinds of religious and linguistic baggage, was originally employed by colonial writers; it was subsequently taken up by proto-nationalist and nationalist intellectuals, and is now a *sine qua non* in popular political rhetoric. In Tamil Nadu, the local brahmins have become the representatives of the northern others and have been the butt of generations of Dravidian nationalists (Barnett 1977; Dirks 1993).

It could be argued that in the twentieth century 'race', in some recognizably Western Victorian sense, has become the dominant motif in the political ethnosociology of Tamil Nadu and Sri Lanka. The embarrassing implications of this neatly expose the limitations of the various sorts of anthropological occidentalism in South Asia. This political use of occidental (and occidentalist) ideas by élite politicians echoes the cases discussed by Herzfeld and by Gewertz and Errington. In particular, it is reminiscent of Herzfeld's Greek élites pursuing ever more inauthentic markers of the genuinely authentic. But it also reveals the limits of the anti-occidentalist project: the racial other in south Indian politics is not the white colonizer but the allegedly northern brahmin, and this other does not live in the West but lives in India. In Sri Lanka the other is either the Tamil or the Sinhala 'invader' (for both sides in the conflict are capable of defining themselves as autochthonous when circumstances demand this) who seeks to displace the pacific natives. I shall discuss the implications of this later.

The politics of occidentalism

It is time to turn away from anthropological arguments about the West and look in more detail at the uses of the image of the West in South Asian politics. This brings me back to the other half of my introduction: the problem of the West in South Asian political and cultural arguments, starting with the Sri Lankan attacks on Western rationality I cited at the start of this chapter. In the newspaper interview I quoted, de Silva, the mathematician, went on to attack the country's universities because of their adherence to Western models and Western ideas. The interviewer asked him if there had not been any 'real intellectuals' in the country, and he replied that there had only been three: Ananda Coomaraswamy, Martin Wickremesinghe, and Munidasa Cumaratunga (*Island* 1991). On the surface the three figures cited have little in common, except that they are all dead, and perhaps more importantly all three have major writings on Sinhala culture and language published and available in Sinhala.[7] These three exemplars can be used to display some of the uses of occidentalism in South Asian cultural politics.

Coomaraswamy is the only one of these figures whose fame extends beyond Sri Lanka. The son of a distinguished Tamil father and an English mother, he was educated in late-Victorian Britain and returned to Sri Lanka at the turn of the century to take up a position in the Ceylon Civil Service. He stayed for four years, when he was active in nationalist and social reform circles, before returning to Britain, where his important study *Medieval Sinhalese Art* was published in 1908; in later years his extensive publications made him the most important single figure in the twentieth-century study of Indian art (Mitter 1977: 277–86). His early publications on Sinhalese culture make frequent comparisons between East and West. In the opening pages of *Medieval Sinhalese Art* Coomaraswamy argues that the 'influence of contact with the West has been fatal to the arts' (Coomaraswamy 1956: p. vi); a combination of commerce and shallow talk of progress have led to the demise of traditional craftsmanship and a debasement of taste. This interpretation is not unlike the version of the West put forward by Herzfeld's craftworkers, but the ultimate moral derived is distinctly un-Thatcherite. Coomaraswamy's West is the West of alienated labour, and his description of the pernicious effects of separating art from labour owes much to the influence of William Morris, on whose Kelmscott Press Coomaraswamy printed the book. Printing such a book on Morris's press was, Coomaraswamy suggested, 'an illustration of the way in which the East and the West may together be united in an endeavour to restore that true Art of Living which has for so long been neglected by humanity' (1956: p. ix).[8]

Coomaraswamy's writings connect to a more obviously radical tradition that combines elements of what I have called romantic and positivist occidentalism. Again, there are the loose equations between the Eastern present and the pre-modern (usually medieval) West, but for Coomaraswamy the pre-modern was a powerful source of social critique. Nevertheless, as

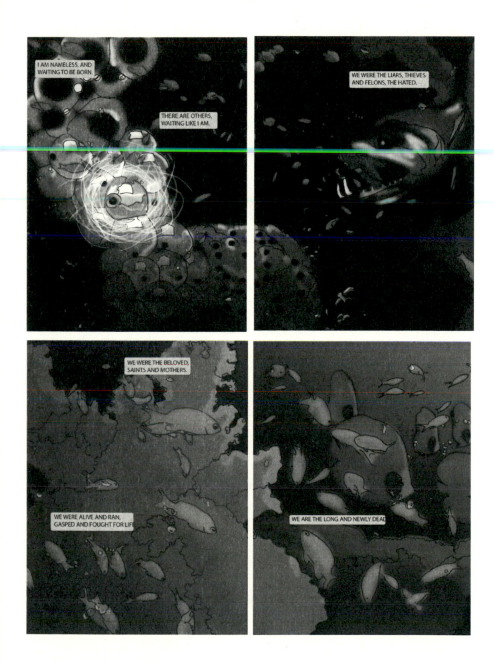

James Brow points out, the absence of conflict and struggle in Coomaraswamy's utopian vision of rural tradition in the East left him closer to Ruskin than to his acknowledged hero Morris (Brow 1992). While Coomaraswamy described a potential temporal unity linking East and West, his critique of 'progress' indicates his suspicion of the modern. In fact Coomaraswamy's use of East–West imagery was complex. Although he argued for a style of cultural pluralism which drew strongly on romantic nationalism, for him Ceylon itself only really stood for the greater whole of the 'motherland', India, while the problem with the impact of the West was that the wrong bits of the West had been received with the most enthusiasm by the emerging indigenous middle class. As in so many of the cases in this book, East and West are ways of talking about the problems of class and consumption.

Coomaraswamy seems to me to embody many of the themes of the earlier chapters in this collection. His ruralism, for example, would seem to draw on the same contrasts—rural vs. urban, traditional vs. modern— as Nadel-Klein's more recent British anthropologists and literary detectives, but with a very different final valuation. In fact, Coomaraswamy was heir to a century's efforts at interpreting, comparing, and evaluating the village life of East and West. Victorian theorists regularly used contemporary Indian (and Russian) evidence to understand what they took to be the European past. In the middle of the nineteenth century, this project was vested with great political urgency; the study of the rural life found alike in the Western past and Eastern present 'once pullulated with contemporary relevance' (Dewey 1972: 293). The same contrast between rural and urban, past and present, could be used to generate completely different political conclusions depending on the predilections of individual writers. Reviewing Maine's *Village Communities East and West*, Tylor commented that 'A peasant village . . . is not a society with progressive tendencies.' Morgan, in contrast, thought that progress lay with a revival of the collective institutions of the past (Dewey 1972: 315). In the case of Thornton's South Africa, occidentalism marks out a particular space as a site of special moral relevance, a place in which we can watch a 'sort of generic passion play that could be equally useful to capitalists or communists, socialists or democrats'. So too, the village community of the East was once used as a kind of political Rorschach from which all observers could draw their own conclusions. The only common factor was the agreement that these conclusions mattered, morally and politically.

Coomaraswamy's ruralism is exemplary for another reason. His vision of the countryside stands at the intersection of positivist occidentalism—

Tylor, Maine, Morgan—and romantic occidentalism. It is also the point at which the occidentalist baton passes from Western anthropology to Eastern nationalists. In Sri Lanka the village community of Victorian social theory lives on as the *fons et origo* of post-colonial political programmes, even as it continues to haunt the ethnographic imagination (Spencer 1992). In the 1920s and 1930s, élite politicians employed a rather carefully tailored image of the archetypal Eastern village in building the ideological foundations of mass politics in Sri Lanka (Samaraweera 1981; Moore 1992). In the 1980s, government programmes sought to rebuild those villages (Brow 1988). My point here, though, is not simply to list another example of élite employment of occidentalist stereotypes in pursuit of élite interests. Gewertz and Errington are right—the contrasts employed by élite politicians are chosen because they are likely to work. Stereotypical contrasts are 'good to use' because they are 'good to think', and they are good to think because they address real predicaments. Again, I will return to this point later.

Cumaratunga, the second of the mathematician's exemplars, provides a strong contrast with Coomaraswamy in almost every possible way. A mid-century linguistic reformer, he was concerned to recover an originary 'pure' Sinhala language, purged of alien Indian elements. Not for him the engagement with the Indian 'motherland' or the creative learning from other cultures. Rather, he posited a radical linguistic fundamentalism, based on a search for an original language, which could make good the debilitating effects of 2,000 years of contact with the Sanskritic traditions of India. The most recent account of Cumaratunga's career makes no mention of the West as a point of orientation in his search for radical authenticity: the others against whom he pitted his polemics were as often as not Buddhist and nationalist leaders who failed his exacting standards of linguistic, and thus cultural, purity (Dharmadasa 1992).

While Cumaratunga's extreme indigenist version of cultural identity failed to attract a mass following, his writings have bequeathed two legacies in the politics of identity in Sri Lanka. One is the possibility of a purely linguistic nationalism which could admit Sinhala Christians as well as Buddhists (Dharmadasa 1992: 286)—a possible source of the mathematician's characterization of the 'Western' world-view as 'Judaic', rather than the more obvious 'Judaeo-Christian', and a further example of what Lindstrom describes as the 'porous' boundary between East and West. The second is a version of contrastive difference in which India replaced the West as the defining other, a version well suited to the geopolitical realities of post-colonial Sri Lanka (Dharmadasa 1992:

281–3). This latter point connects with the Dravidian movement in south India—the emergence of which was almost exactly coeval with Cumaratunga's parallel activities in Sri Lanka—whose other was again not the West, but brahminic north India. The point here is important: even in the last decades of colonial rule, the major political and cultural cleavages were not necessarily those between colonizer and colonized. Half a century later this is even more the case, and we need to be even more wary of reducing all the world's politics to the contrast between the West and the Rest, however perversely flattering such a contrast may be for those who live and work in the West.

My third example, Martin Wickremesinghe, was a prolific novelist and journalist whose career spanned the decades before and after Independence. His nationalist vision of Sinhala culture, like Coomaraswamy's, extolled the virtues of the rural peasant while criticizing the deracinated tastes of the Westernized bourgeoisie. Again the contrast is the same as Nadel-Klein discusses, but the values are different. On language, like Cumaratunga but in milder tones, Wickremesinghe criticized the unnecessary use of Sanskritic elements in modern Sinhala. But, also like Coomaraswamy, Wickremesinghe was by no means opposed to the West as such; he was a socialist humanist, an early expounder of Darwin in Sinhala, and an avid reader of cultural anthropology (cf. Spencer 1990). His use of an anthropological concept of culture allowed him to celebrate cultural borrowings as a sign of creativity and vitality while decrying futile attempts to breathe life into dead traditions: what was distinctive about a culture, he argued, was not the individual elements, but their distinctive configuration or genius (Wickremesinghe 1992). In his later writings, however, he seems to have become less confident about the creative potential of intercultural borrowing, complaining about the dangers of shallow cultural 'imitation' which would only lead to 'unintegrated' culture and 'rootlessness' (Wickremesinghe 1975). These later writings are increasingly pessimistic about the prospects for Sinhala culture, and the contradictions between his progressivist attachment to science and his romantic nostalgia for the disappearing rural order become increasingly evident and unresolved. He seems to have become more and more aware of two pressing imperatives: the need for a sense of authenticity and its utter impossibility. The paradox is similar to those explored by Herzfeld in his contribution to this volume. Nevertheless, the butt of Wickremesinghe's criticisms was almost never the 'West', but the 'Westernized', in other words the Sri Lankan bourgeoisie. His occidentalism, if such it was, was again part of a critique of internal class differences within Sri Lanka.

Viewed in the cold light of dogmatic anti-essentialism, all three of my Sri Lankan exemplars fail to make the grade. Coomaraswamy, like Gandhi, taps into what Richard Fox (1989) cunningly calls 'affirmative Orientalism' and, like Gandhi (and Dumont), uses the idea of the West as a way of talking about the modern, even as he draws on Western critics of modernity for inspiration. Cumaratunga engages in an impossibly quixotic search for linguistic purity and a lost literary and cultural heritage; his other, though, is Indian rather than Western. Wickremesinghe attempts to celebrate an openness to Western ideas even as he laments the shallowness of rootless borrowings; he ends up a prisoner of an impossible quest for authenticity. In all three cases, to differing extents, the writers are not simply writing against the West (in the person of the colonizer), but they are also writing against some of their fellow Sri Lankans. Between them, we have a reasonably representative selection of the predicaments and possibilities still open to the post-colonial intellectual.

A strong version of the occidentalist structure of feeling has recently reappeared in the work of the Indian social critic Ashis Nandy, whose fierce denunciation of Nehru's vision of a secular India draws on both Gandhi and the cultural pessimism of the Frankfurt school. Nandy employs the same binary contrasts we might find in Dumont: East to West as traditional to modern as religious to secular. His affirmative orientalism involves revaluing the East, such that the traditional, rural, and religious are the proper sites of tolerance and humanity (Nandy 1990). His attempt to challenge the hegemony of Western scientific and technocratic reason has obvious parallels in the Sri Lankan efforts of the Jathika Chintanaya intellectuals, as well as shared roots in what Thornton calls an occidentalism of 'external recourse'. In nineteenth-century South Africa a benign West which could be reasonably expected to intercede locally was symbolized by Christianity and the Queen. Nandy's 'other West', in contrast, is the West of those utopian critics of industrial society who inspired Gandhi and Coomaraswamy. And Nandy's comments on Gandhi's non-relativism and his debts to Western thinkers apply to both Coomaraswamy and Wickremesinghe, as well as to Nandy himself (Nandy 1992: 127–9; cf. Appadurai 1988).

There is no sense in any of this that the West can, or should, be denied as a cultural presence in India or Sri Lanka. This style of occidentalism is radically different, then, from the work of those anthropologists like Dumont and Marriott whose version of the real India is purged of inauthentic Western ideas, and closer to Thornton's South Africans whose West continues to bear the traces of the complex history of which it is a product. What Nandy, like his predecessors, is trying to do is sift out those aspects of the West which he sees as inimical to a humane society: if the West cannot be denied, nevertheless it must be dealt with.[9] The nineteenth-century evolution from the Eastern past to the Western present is a recurring possibility in Nandy's writing, only now it is presented as a threat to be avoided rather than a necessity to be embraced. 'The younger sibling', as Carrier puts it in his Introduction, 'can see and speak the truth about the elder.'

Seen from the East, then, the uses of occidentalism seem rather different. It follows that we must be especially wary of dismissing the arguments of colonial and post-colonial intellectuals in the name, not of occidentalist authenticity, but of anti-essentialist or historicist authenticity: the rural was never like that, this is not *kastom* it is invention, and so on. So when James Clifford, commenting on Said, suggests that 'all dichotomizing concepts should probably be held in suspicion' and 'we should attempt to think of cultures not as organically unified or traditionally continuous but rather as negotiated, present processes' (Clifford 1988: 273), we should also remember that the 'we' he is primarily addressing is an audience of anthropologists and related Western intellectuals. Loose talk of the West to an audience of Western anthropologists invokes a questionable rhetoric of authenticity which seems to deny the real historical connections which have shaped society and culture in the disparate world of the non-West. Clifford is indeed right to caution against academic dichotomizing.

But there are problems with the rhetoric of historicist, anti-essentialist authenticity. Other people's dichotomies may serve different purposes from anthropological dichotomies. When anthropologists talk about the West, their occidentalism is not, on the whole, connected to any attempt to imagine a form of political community, except that odd Groucho Marx intellectual community that is the anthropologist's occident: a club we would not join if it would have us as members. But other people's dichotomies and essentialisms take life in different political contexts. Not the least of their purposes is the invocation of solidarity amongst an 'us', a group of people who feel themselves otherwise powerless in the face of what they think of as the West. Other people's essentialisms are, amongst other things, often crucial components in attempts to re-imagine or re-build forms of community and solidarity which they feel are needed to deal with the West they experience. Clifford invokes an idea of 'negotiation' in his reformulation of cultural difference, but it is so much easier to negotiate from a position of power.

Clifford describes the West as 'a force . . . no longer radiating in any simple way from a discrete geographical or cultural center' (Clifford 1988: 272). But the point, for many post-colonial intellectuals, is that wherever it comes from, the force we call the West comes from outside wherever it is they live, and Clifford's scrupulously abstract and depersonalized West may itself owe too much to one rather recent and specific image of the modern: 'sorry we had to shut the plant and move production to Singapore, this is the transnational world in which we live.' At the recent ASA Oxford Conference on globalization, the most vociferous opposition to the analytic abolition of the West came, of course, from non-Western anthropologists, and the substance of their objections was compelling: if it is not the West, what is it that swamps our domestic markets, fills our television and radio broadcasts, and sets our academic agendas?

Somewhere along this line, it is possible to rejoin anthropological attempts at cultural criticism. Mauss's essay on *The Gift* was as much a critique of modernity as a celebration of it, and even Dumont's work has some explicit moral charge in reminding the reader that he or she is not a monadic individual but a properly social being. What I have called the rhetoric of authenticity has its immediate anthropological roots in the 1920s: in Sapir's contrast between the spiritual desert inhabited by the 'telephone girl' and the fulfilment of the 'Indian' spearing salmon, or in Mead's insouciant diagnosis of the ills of American education, armed with all the authority of one who has been elsewhere (Sapir 1924; cf. Stocking 1988). And it takes little effort to connect those early anthropological critiques of modernity to what Nandy calls the 'other West' and its internal critique of industrial society.

I feel uneasy about a simple endorsement of Nandy's position and I feel equally uneasy about simply dismissing his arguments on anti-occidentalist grounds. But if I claim that it all looks different from the perspective of the colonized world, there is the further danger of homogenizing the post-colonial condition into an uncritical apologia for the 'strategic essentialisms' of authentic post-colonials.[10] Yet, as I have argued, there is a very real difference in the political context of contemporary anthropological occidentalisms and more or less indigenous South Asian occidentalisms. In the end, anthropological occidentalisms posit a radical difference between 'us' or the 'West', and 'them'. Without this difference, the authenticity and power of our versions of them would be lessened: our ideas would be less challenging, our reports less striking, our authority compromised. But South Asian occidentalisms seem to me to make little attempt to deny the very real impact of the West on South Asian social life: indeed they derive much of their rhetorical force from their authors' awareness of the scale and human cost of that impact. In India and Sri Lanka, as in anthropology, the trope of the West subsumes, and in many cases stands for, the other great divides in the human sciences: urban vs. rural, science vs. religion, modern vs. traditional. But it is also a mnemonic for the historical experience of colonial rule, a way to criticize the unjust distribution of cultural resources in deeply unequal societies, and it may be actively employed in attempts to build alternative visions of a political community, in which people retain the power to make some of their own cultural choices in a world in which such areas of autonomy seem to be forever eroding.

The education of desire

Let me offer a few tentative conclusions to this whole volume. One harks back to Coomaraswamy's critique of the debased taste of the emerging Sri Lankan middle class. This reminds us that, for many of the people discussed in the chapters of this book, the West is not primarily encountered as a discourse, an epistemology, or even a politics, let alone a real place with real people. The West is encountered in the form of things, items of consumption and objects of desire. It occurs to me that the whole book could, with only minor editorial changes, be re-presented as a series of case-studies in the politics of consumption.

This theme links Coomaraswamy's village artisans to Herzfeld's craftworkers, to Creighton's fantasy excursions, and of course to Lindstrom's clinical analysis of the many ways we all talk of cargo. Melanesia, for the anthropologists Carrier discusses, is the society of the gift, and gifts are above all not commodities. Lindstrom concludes by suggesting a hidden hegemonic assumption running through the discourse of cargoism: the assumption 'that a human desire that is never satisfied and never-ending is the normal, truthful experience of humankind everywhere'. James Brow, whose interpretation of Coomaraswamy partly inspired this chapter, ends that interpretation with some words from E. P. Thompson's defence of utopianism in his biography of William Morris. In imagining alternatives 'our habitual values (the "commonsense" of bourgeois society) are thrown into disarray. And we enter into Utopia's proper and new-found space: the education of desire' (Thompson quoted in Brow 1992). That is one enduring use of the idea of the West, explicit in the Gandhian critique of modernity: the West as an aid in the utopian attempt to educate desire. If this collection needs a new subtitle, it could be 'Chapters in the Education of Desire'; sometimes this education leads away from the hegemonic assumptions discussed by Lindstrom, sometimes—and Creighton's chapter is a good example—it represents more of an attempt to smooth away the differences between local expectations of harmony and systemic requirements for egotistical hunger.

For much of this chapter I have relied on a simple contrast of my own—between the anthropologists who deny (or at least ignore) the ties of colonial history, and the intellectuals from sometime-colonized places who use the image of the West as a way of coming to terms with it. The chapters in this book make a valuable start in the necessary shift away from a concern with occidentalist discourse, to inspection of the political contexts in which that discourse is used. Even so, there is a long way to go in our interpretation of those contexts, and it is important to acknowledge that there is more to post-colonial politics than the machiavellian manipulations of élite politicians, just as the political sociology of the post-colonial world is somewhat more complex than a simple division between élites (or bourgeoisies) and the rest might suggest. Occidentalist discourse is both 'good to think' and 'good to use': it appeals because it makes some sort of sense of broad predicaments shared to some extent by politicians, intellectuals, and ordinary people.

Finally, though, we need to recognize the limits of our chosen subject. Occidentalism is a convenient label under which to examine a range of responses to colonialism and modernity. I have already suggested that the comparative themes that have emerged from this book belie the argument that anthropological comparison is impossible without the kind of gross totalizing images of the West I discussed in the opening section. Those images are part of our language of persuasion, not part of our empirical procedures. What the comparisons in this book provide is above all a set of histories of the production of moral spaces. Some of these areas of heightened moral imagination are real enough—South Africa for example. Others are only too obviously imagined—the village community or the Western mind. But we also have to recognize that there are other zones of heightened moral imagination which slip through the net of our concern with occidentalism, just as there are other others. In Sri Lanka, the West takes a back seat to the Tamil or the Sinhala, Hindu, Muslim, or Buddhist, as the crucial contrast to the self. In India it is again the Muslim or the Hindu, the northern brahmin and the southern Dravidian. These terms have colonial histories, but it is flattery of a peculiar perversity to reduce them now to the binary opposition between colonizer and colonized, West and East, occident and orient. There are always yet more complex stories out there waiting to be told.

Acknowledgements

This chapter has benefited from the critical comments of Janet Carsten, Chris Fuller, colleagues from the Centre for South Asian Studies in Edinburgh, and students from my postgraduate writing group. James Carrier not only pushed me to write it in the first place, he also forced me to try to turn an argument about Sri Lanka into a conclusion to this book. The flaws and simplifications are mine, the stimulus was his.

Notes

1 The group itself insists on the untranslatability of 'chintanaya', which from their position is precisely the point: even their name is testimony to the unique genius of Sinhala culture. My colleague Paul Dundas tells me that, in fact, 'cintanaya' is an unremarkable Sanskrit term for 'that which should be known'. For simplicity's sake I have retained the newspaper transliteration of what would otherwise be 'jatika cintanaya'.

2 At the same time, the other key figure in the movement, the novelist Amarasekera, dismissed multiculturalism as 'a cocktail' (*Sunday Observer* 1991).

3 To be fair, Kapferer acknowledges the presence of 'modern' or 'Western' traits like individualism in some areas of life in Sri Lanka (Kapferer 1988: 79–80), but the main thrust of his argument is the analysis of a common cultural 'logic' at the heart of the old chronicles and in the hearts of contemporary zealots, and this analysis in turn rests on repeated contrasts with the West and Western rationalism (1988: 140–1).

4 Kapferer's comparison is based on a much more demotic understanding of the West than either Dumont or Marriott; even so, his discussion of mateship and egalitarian values in Australia is far thinner and less ethnographically nuanced than e.g. his own earlier work on healing rituals in Sri Lanka (cf. Kapferer 1983).

5 This position is explicit in the title of the last section of Dumont's introduction to *Homo Hierarchicus*, 'The necessity of hierarchy' (Dumont 1980: 19–20), and in his comparison of caste and racism (1980: 247–66).

6 In India, Dumont's version of caste and South Asian society has most often been criticized not from a culturological, but from a Marxist, position. A proper consideration of occidentalism in South Asian Marxism is beyond the scope of this chapter.

7 Cumaratunga's major writings are only available in Sinhala; Wickremesinghe wrote and published extensively in both Sinhala and English; a Sinhala translation of Coomaraswamy's only major work on Sinhala culture, *Medieval Sinhalese Art*, was sponsored by the government after Independence. My interpretation of Coomaraswamy is heavily dependent on so-far unpublished research by James Brow, while my comments on Cumaratunga are based on K. N. O. Dharmadasa (1992: 261–89).

8 Morris is also repeatedly quoted in Coomaraswamy's *An Open Letter to the Kandyan Chiefs*, dating from the same period, calling for the preservation of traditional architecture (Coomaraswamy 1957).

9 The question, of course, remains of assessing Nandy's controversial vision of the politics of post-colonial culture. My own problem is less with his discussions of the West *per se*, as with his polemical simplifications of what are much more complex historical processes. Like other critics, I also have difficulties with his vision of the rural and his uncritical stance toward the traditional (cf. Appadurai 1988; Uyangoda 1991).

10 The phrase is Gayatri Spivak's (in Appiah 1992: 341 n. 4).

References

APPADURAI, ARJUN (1988). 'Is Homo Hierarchicus?' *American Ethnologist*, 15: 745–61.

APPIAH, KWAME A. (1992). *In my Father's House: What Does it Mean to be an African Today?* London: Methuen.

BAILEY, F. G. (1959). 'For a Sociology of India?' *Contributions to Indian Sociology*, 3: 88–101.

BARNETT, STEVE (1977). 'Identity Choice and Caste Ideology in Contemporary South India', in Kenneth David (ed.), *The New Wind: Changing Identities in South Asia*. The Hague: Mouton: 393–416.

BÉTEILLE, ANDRÉ (1983). 'Homo Hierarchicus, Homo Equalis', in A. Béteille, *The Idea of Natural Inequality and Other Essays*. Delhi: Oxford University Press: 33–53.

——(1990). 'Race, Caste and Gender', *Man*, 25: 489–504.

BROW, JAMES (1988). 'In Pursuit of Hegemony: Representations of Authority and Justice in a Sri Lankan Village', *American Ethnologist*, 15: 311–27.

——(1992). 'The Education of Desire: Images of the Village Community in the Early Writings of Ananda Coomaraswamy', unpublished MS.

CARRIER, JAMES G. (1992). 'Occidentalism: The World Turned Upside-Down', *American Ethnologist*, 19: 195–212.

CLIFFORD, JAMES (1988). 'On Orientalism', in J. Clifford, *The Predicament of Culture: Twentieth-Century Ethnography, Literature, and Art*. Cambridge, Mass.: Harvard University Press: 255–76.

COOMARASWAMY, ANANDA K. (1956 [1908]). *Medieval Sinhalese Art*. (2nd edn.) New York: Pantheon.

——(1957 [1905]). *An Open Letter to the Kandyan Chiefs*. Colombo: Arts Council of Ceylon.

DEWEY, CLIVE (1972). 'Images of the Village Community: A Study in Anglo-Indian Ideology', *Modern Asian Studies*, 6: 291–328.

DHARMADASA, K. N. O. (1992). *Language, Religion, and Ethnic Assertiveness: The Growth of Sinhalese Nationalism in Sri Lanka*. Ann Arbor, Mich.: University of Michigan Press.

WE ARE THE WAITING.

THE SUN RISES FROM THE NOTHING, AND I FEEL ITS COMFORT ON MY FACE AND ARMS.

THE ICE SINKING IN MY WATER WARS WITH THE HEAT, AND ITS BLOOD GATHERS ON THE GLASS AND SPILLS DOWN THE SIDES.

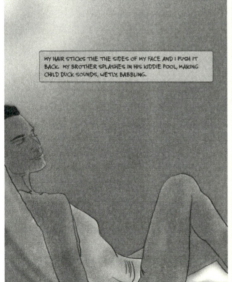

MY HAIR STICKS THE THE SIDES OF MY FACE AND I PUSH IT BACK. MY BROTHER SPLASHES IN HIS KIDDIE POOL, MAKING CHILD DUCK SOUNDS, WETLY, BABBLING.

OUR PARENTS FIGHT INSIDE THE HOUSE AND I ROLL OVER TO TAN MY BACK.

THE WORLD SWIMS AWAY FROM ME.

256 *Jonathan Spencer*

DIRKS, NICHOLAS B. (1993). 'Recasting Tamil Society: The Politics of Caste, Race, and Ethnicity in Contemporary Southern India', unpublished MS.

DOUGLAS, MARY (1972). 'Introduction to Paladin Edition', in Louis Dumont, *Homo Hierarchicus: The Caste System and its Implications*. London: Paladin: 11–22.

DUMONT, LOUIS (1980 [1966]). *Homo Hierarchicus: The Caste System and its Implications*, rev. edn. Chicago: University of Chicago Press.

——and POCOCK, DAVID (1957). 'For a Sociology of India', *Contributions to Indian Sociology*, 1: 7–22.

FABIAN, JOHANNES (1983). *Time and the Other: How Anthropology Makes its Object*. New York: Columbia University Press.

FOX, RICHARD G. (1989). *Gandhian Utopia: Experiments with Culture*. Boston: Beacon Press.

GALEY, JEAN-CLAUDE (1991). 'Louis Dumont', in Pierre Bonte and Michel Izard (eds.), *Dictionnaire de l'ethnologie et de l'anthropologie*. Paris: Presses Universitaires de France: 204–6.

Island (1991). 'Sinhala Buddhism: Core of National Culture' (interview with Nalin de Silva), *Island* (20 July).

KAPFERER, BRUCE (1983). *A Celebration of Demons: Exorcism and the Aesthetics of Healing in Sri Lanka*. Bloomington, Ind.: Indiana University Press.

——(1988). *Legends of People, Myths of State: Violence, Intolerance, and Political Culture in Sri Lanka and Australia*. Washington, DC: Smithsonian Institution Press.

KEMPER, STEVEN (1991). *The Presence of the Past: Chronicles, Politics, and Culture in Sinhala Life*. Ithaca, NY: Cornell University Press.

KUMAR, NITA (1992). *Friends, Brothers, and Informants: Fieldwork Memoirs of Banaras*. Berkeley, Calif.: University of California Press.

LÉVI-STRAUSS, CLAUDE (1969). *The Elementary Structures of Kinship*. London: Tavistock.

MARRIOTT, McKIM (1990a). 'Introduction', in M. Marriott (ed.), *India through Hindu Categories*. Delhi: Sage: pp. xi–xvi.

——(1990b). 'Constructing an Indian Ethnosociology', in M. Marriott (ed.), *India through Hindu Categories*. Delhi: Sage: 1–39.

——and INDEN, RONALD (1977). 'Toward an Ethnosociology of South Asian Caste Systems', in Kenneth David (ed.), *The New Wind: Changing Identities in South Asia*. The Hague: Mouton: 227–38.

MAUSS, MARCEL (1985 [1938]). 'A Category of the Human Mind: The Notion of Person; the Notion of Self', in Michael Carrithers, Steven Collins, and Steven Lukes (eds.), *The Category of the Person*. Cambridge: Cambridge University Press: 1–25.

——(1990 [1925]). *The Gift: The Form and Reason for Exchange in Archaic Societies*, trans. W. D. Halls. London: Routledge.

MITTER, PARTHA (1977). *Much Maligned Monsters: History of European Reactions to Indian Art*. Oxford: Clarendon Press.

MOORE, MICK P. (1992). 'The Ideological History of the Sri Lankan "Peasantry"', in James Brow and Joe Weeramunda (eds.), *Agrarian Change in Sri Lanka*. New Delhi: Sage: 326–56.

NANDY, ASHIS (1990). 'The Politics of Secularism and the Recovery of Religious Tolerance', in Veena Das (ed.), *Mirrors of Violence: Communities, Riots and Survivors in South Asia*. Delhi: Oxford University Press: 127–62.

——(1992). 'From outside the Imperium: Gandhi's Cultural Critique of the West', in A. Nandy, *Traditions, Tyranny, and Utopias: Essays in the Politics of Awareness*. Delhi: Oxford University Press: 69–93.

ROGERS, JOHN D. (1990). 'Historical Images in the British Period', in Jonathan Spencer (ed.), *Sri Lanka: History and the Roots of Conflict*. London: Routledge: 87–106.

SAMARAWEERA, VIJAYA (1981). 'Land, Labor, Capital and Sectional Interests in the National Politics of Sri Lanka', *Modern Asian Studies*, 15: 127–62.

SAPIR, EDWARD (1924). 'Culture, Genuine and Spurious', *American Journal of Sociology*, 29: 401–29.

SPENCER, JONATHAN (1990). 'Writing within: Anthropology, Nationalism and Culture in Sri Lanka', *Current Anthropology*, 31: 283–91.

——(1992). 'Representations of the Rural: A View from Sabaragamuva', in James Brow and J. Weeramunda (eds.), *Agrarian Change in Sri Lanka*. New Delhi: Sage: 357–87.

STOCKING, GEORGE (1988). 'The Ethnographic Sensibility of the 1920s and the Dualism of the Anthropological Tradition', in G. Stocking (ed.), *Romantic Motives*. History of Anthropology 6. Madison, Wis.: University of Wisconsin Press: 208–76.

STRATHERN, MARILYN (1988). *The Gender of the Gift: Problems with Women and Problems with Society in Melanesia*. Berkeley, Calif.: University of California Press.

Sunday Observer (1991). 'Fears of JC Leading to Violence Unfounded' (interview with Gunadasa Amarasekera), *Sunday Observer* (7 July).

TENNEKOON, SERENA (1990). 'Newspaper Nationalism: Sinhala Identity as Historical Discourse', in Jonathan Spencer (ed.), *Sri Lanka: History and the Roots of Conflict*. London: Routledge: 205–26.

UYANGODA, JAYDEVA (1991). 'Review of *Mirrors of Violence*', *Lanka Guardian* (15 Mar.): 31–2; (1 May): 27–9.

WICKREMESINGHE, MARTIN (1975). *Sinhala Language and Culture*. Dehiwela: Tissa Prakasakayo.

——(1992 [1952]). *Aspects of Sinhalese Culture*. (4th edn.) Dehiwela: Tissa Prakasakayo.

NOTES ON CONTRIBUTORS

JAMES G. CARRIER has made extensive study of Melanesian society in collaboration with his wife, Aschah Carrier; they are joint authors of *Wage, Trade, and Exchange in Melanesia* (1989) and *Structure and Process in a Melanesian Society* (1991). He is also the author of *Gifts and Commodities: Exchange and Western Capitalism since 1700* (1994), and the editor of *History and Tradition in Melanesian Anthropology* (1992). He currently teaches anthropology at Durham University.

MILLIE R. CREIGHTON teaches anthropology, sociology, and Japanese studies at the University of British Columbia; her research has focused particularly on various consumer-oriented industries in Japan.

FREDERICK K. ERRINGTON is Charles A. Dana Professor of Anthropology at Trinity College, Connecticut. He is the author of *Karavar: Masks and Power in a Melanesian Ritual* (1974) and *Manners and Meaning in West Sumatra* (1984). He is co-author with his wife, Deborah Gewertz, of *Cultural Histories and a Feminist Anthropology* (1987), *Twisted Histories, Altered Contexts: Representing the Chambri in a World System* (1991), and *Articulating Change in the Last Unknown* (forthcoming).

DEBORAH B. GEWERTZ is Professor of Anthropology at Amherst College, Massachusetts. She is the author of numerous articles about Papua New Guinea, and the book *Sepik River Societies* (1983). She is co-author with Frederick Errington of the three works listed above.

MICHAEL HERZFELD is Professor of Anthropology at Harvard University and editor of *American Ethnologist*. He has been president of the Society for the Anthropology of Europe and of the Modern Greek Studies Association. His books include *Anthropology through the Looking-Glass: Critical Ethnography in the Margins of Europe* (1987), *A Place in History: Social and Monumental Time in a Cretan Town* (1991), and *The Social Production of Indifference: Exploring the Symbolic Roots of Western Bureaucracy* (1992).

LAMONT LINDSTROM is Professor and Chair of the Department of Anthropology at the University of Tulsa. He specializes in the south-west

Pacific, and has published on island knowledge systems, linguistics, and ethnohistory. His most recent book is *Cargo Cult: Strange Stories of Desire from Melanesia and beyond* (1993).

JANE NADEL-KLEIN has published articles on localism and identity in Scotland, and is co-editor of a book on women in fishing communities, *To Work and to Weep* (1988). She is Associate Professor of Anthropology at Trinity College, Connecticut.

DEBORAH REED-DANAHAY is an assistant professor in the Department of Anthropology and Sociology at the University of Texas, Arlington. Her primary interests are the anthropology of education, political anthropology, personal narrative, and social theory. In addition to having written *Les Notres: Schooling, Identity and Resistance in Rural France* (1995), she has published several articles in France and the United States.

JONATHAN SPENCER is Senior Lecturer in Social Anthropology at the University of Edinburgh. He is the author of *A Sinhala Village in a Time of Trouble* (1990) and the editor of *Sri Lanka: History and the Roots of Conflict* (1990).

ROBERT THORNTON took anthropology degrees at Stanford and the University of Chicago, then taught anthropology at the University of Cape Town from 1978 to 1989; he is now Associate Professor and Head of the Department of Social Anthropology at the University of the Witwatersrand, Johannesburg. His publications include *Space, Time and Culture among the Iraqw of Tanzania* (1980) and *The Early Writings of Bronislaw Malinowski, 1904–1914* (1992).

INDEX

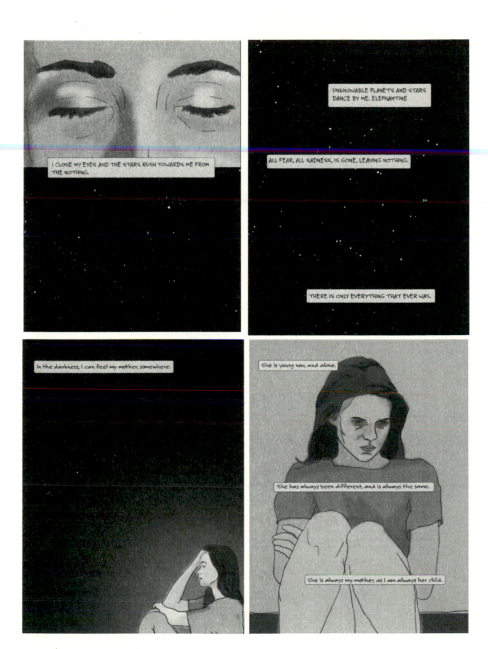

Index